Stems from the Edge of Silence

Writings from the springs of the mind

HANNA ABI AKL

Stems from the Edge of Silence
Copyright © 2020 by Hanna Abi Akl
Waterton Publishing Company

All rights reserved. No part of this book may be reproduced, stored, or transmitted by any means—whether auditory, graphic, mechanical,or electronic—without written permission of the author, except in the case of brief excerpts used in critical articles and reviews. Unauthorized reproduction of any part of this work is illegal and is punishable by law.

Because of the dynamic nature of the Internet, any web addresses or links contained in this book may have changed since publication and may no longer be valid. The views expressed in this work are solely those of the author and do not necessarily reflect the views of the publisher, and the publisher hereby disclaims any responsibility for them.

ISBN 978-1-7347632-0-1

watertonpublishing.com

Contents

One	1
Two	19
Three	37
Four	97
Five	153
Six	215

One

*Poetry is the holy verse
all else is blasphemy*

i bought her flowers

i bought her flowers
changed water, put them in vase
on the porch they hang

bathed in cold sunlight
holding space-time together
the white ones open

i sigh of relief
she loves the white flowers best
i point them to her

yet she refuses to look.

on the act of kindness

here i am now; rolling with
the wind; beating ceaselessly
against the mad centuries

progress has been lost
humanity ranks first in
slavery; last in kindness

i have reached a point
where i dish out niceties
and expect none in return

i work in reverse
against the clock of this lost
civilization

i do not honk at others
i let them go through

nor do i direct insults
at the waiter; i hand him
his tip with my chin held high

it pains me the serviceman
has to brace himself
and be ready at all times
to be confronted,
put down, provoked, lambasted

by those who are still afraid

if we keep aiming this low
then we truly have no chance

the last of us will be torn
up like thin paper

gamblers, idiots alike
will be wasted and dried out
like scarecrows in a corn field

hollowed out and forgotten.

security

it is a book in my coat
it travels with me
everywhere i go

knowing it is there
even if i don't read it.

cartoon mania

i miss this other planet
waking at 5 in the morn
to watch animated toons
hear little sister's footsteps
in the corridor
father preparing coffee
mother still tucked in her sheets
he wakes her gently
time to get the kids ready
for school; she stretches her arms
the sun stretches over them
like a well-crafted portrait

i go back to my cartoons
the bottom of the tv
flashes 6 a.m.

the school bus is here
big yellow painted-over
bumpy seats, noisy children
all in uniform

the girls untucking their shirts
looking at the boys
challenging them to chase them
when the bell rings after class
catching them by the shirt tip

i loved chasing them
each day a new girl
to give them all a fair chance

coming back home to mother
preparing sponge bath
washing off dust, dirt and sand
i want to tell her
don't wash the girl scents
from my bo-dy fra-gran-ces
tickling my nostrils

mother wraps head in blanket
like a shawl; father arrives
in his strained work-suit

sun down, 6 p.m.
family dinner
power cut, no light
father says things will brighten…
mother nods, says it's bedtime

i pass the television
on my way to the bedroom
stare at the blank screen
my reflection pale and frail

i think of cartoons
look for tomorrow
and another episode.

adulation

i am unfaithful
an un-believer
walking on immortal ground
alone biting human fruit
of adultery and sin

under the soul-crushing wounds
i wish to believe
in a spiritual world

i follow the voice
to the highest peak
words descending from above

poetry is the holy
verse all else is blasphemy

it is there, it is always
there, lurking in the shadows
the divide of life and death
appearing behind
the curtain of completion

against religion
against oppression
against tyranny

the eye of the beholder

passed on like a torch

even when we banish it

    it is always
    there.

time & distance

darling, don't think i forgot
the days spent evading crowds
swapping rosy avenue
walks for apartment hunting
in arduous winter cold

and coming back short of breath
your arms locked in mine
panting: pant pant pant
unable to count our tracks

to a small house with no bed
sleeping on a broken couch

heads touching the dirty floor
when we couldn't manage to
keep them hanging in mid-air

same sweaty, greasy outfits

eating cereal for days
watching your eyes break
hiding tired breaths

rejecting the days
spitting at the better life
that drove us into this hole
mocking myself in writing,

in the mirror; dwarfed by life
before you, before your eyes

every defeated man knows
how hard it is to bounce back

there is no one else like you
not because you were there with
me; but because you still are.

the wild

deep in forest trees
the wild is too fast for me
perusing me to enter
my loins screaming out:

i am nature's friend
but not its equal.

snake bite

on my arm, poison lingers
does not mix with blood
the beast is slai-n

left its mark like a symbol
put down in two chops
the head flung somewhere

the body, meanwhile
lay here, coiling restlessly
evoking my startling fears

did i kill the thing?
the tail still taunting

is the viper dead?
hisses from the ground
like a child's whispers at night
coming from the next bedroom

i look at the head
de-ca-pi-ta-ted
roll it with my boot

the tongue unfolds from the mouth.

my paris

playing in the sky
fiddling with the horizon
scaling the Eiffel

the city below
like a rampant living thing
exploding, beaming

Paris, my lover
de-claw the laws from your art
let me float with you

give up your rigid
self let your museums speak
listen to your heart

open your arms wide
accept your immigrant sons
like hopeful bastards

answering their call
vocation, venture, passion
you, at their center.

haikus

i feel like speaking
yet the words hardly come by
they fail me always

like a volcano
mostly effusive, dormant
easy words are hard

no matter, i shan't
give up on them, i won't yield
the right ones will come.

mother called today

mother called today
said how is work in paris?
it's good ma, i said.

how is the weather?
did you put on your thick coat?
you could catch a cold.

i'm twenty-six, ma.
goodbye, she said, and hung up.
tomorrow she'd call again.

Two

*Those of us worth saving
left this place long a-go*

homeland

there are those that cry out for
nationalism
the defense of their homeland

home has never been four walls
for me; location is bare

it's what you put, you create
that makes it what it should be

materialistic structures
aren't meant to last
soon enough the world
will be colonized

the question that begs:
where will your home be?

purgatory

fighting alley fights
brawling afternoons
lead to sobering evenings
of regret; cold beer brings back
bittersweet odes of lifetimes
when we ran with the hunted

when wars were not raged by men
when church bells did not cover
voices of reason
when money was still spent on
preserving not destroying

drinking on my own
to this past life colored by
an altered reality
my car waits for me
to trudge back to it
after another beating
behind an alley

lips parted in half
bleeding of human remorse
sighing, knowing there's no end
to it all; more suffering
must come before salvation.

humans (read two ways)

i am not like them
i will bide my time
pray the chaplet every day
— mother used to do it twice —
before i become human
to enter this race again
i am not ready

poem of the mind

poem of the mind
red emerald on the coast
cyclone in my heart

poem of the mind
beating heart in loneliness
agony of mine

rowing in deep sea, aloof
poem of the mind
last candle drop burns all night

crying girl's tears form sand rings
poem of the mind
under star ga-zers

her foot acute while she sleeps
next to me in frosted air
poem of the mind

lost agent in wilderness
sucked in by darkening love
poem of the mind.

outline

i am quiet with others
i am bad at expression
i roar on paper
it's my element

baudelaire holds up his wi-cked
flowers of evil
as the verses melt
blend into a scarf
i wear on my neck
an un-european man
spilling his volatile life
on ink; and ink on paper

the pencil is my cradle
graphite my ammo
i hear key strums while i write
the invisible piano
tracing my every breath
from life into revery

sadness glitches what is real
makes it hard to discern things
how can i feel sunsets now
after loss, mourning, grievance?

grief is my relief

keeps me in touch with the page
my only way back to this
to people, society

if you must learn something here
let it be this: outcasts are
never chosen, they are made.

customers

born a customer
bred a customer

everything is bought and sold
and nothing is made of gold

who agreed to this?
when did we agree to this?
why did we agree to this?

light fire

light fire in children's eyes
playing on the monkey bars
in the public park

subjected to pain and loss
early on in life
wonder how they would react?

maybe go on with living
caught in their sandbox
weaving sand into safewalls

some ride it out and make it
and some turn to dark matter
carry the bottle and run

skip the holy path
of learn, work and raise

blow up in a haze

no easy matter
to let spirit rot
and decay

befriend and adopt the drink
the winos gather around
you're unsure who they prefer

you, or the bottle of Jack?

old friends shed your skin
worry, forget, deny you

they cross you by chance:
are you beaten? depressed? lost?
dejected? suicidal?
faithless? drunk? writing?

who in the hell wants to know?

i am still running.

aspirin

full of life's musings
ar-ray of hope, evergreen
outside, bash and mash

crisis spreads like filth
on every housefloor
even those with dusted rags

world is in turmoil
broadcasters declaring wars
poor bums on subway lines starve

animals don't envy us
their eyes are telling
we can live, they can outlast

little bird, won't you fly me
out of this dark hole?

trick room

in french literature class
thinking of Shawshank prison
of a great escape
begging for a line
writing down the great poets
their illustrious careers

hugo's head ominously
hanging from the centerpiece
the class becomes a trick room
morphs into a dark retreat

i jitter in my seat each
time someone else speaks —
uninterested in what
they have to discuss

attentive to the poets
waiting for one of them to
surge out from his lines
and say: drop everything and
follow me on the journey
of the unknown from here on
out; you will be baptized time
and time again when you write

the first time you will shed blood

but you will escape
from this class; from these curious individuals
hold my hand and jump!

and so i leap from my seat
shouting: i have it — the gift
i have it at last!
the teacher scolds me
but i jump higher
scaring her out of the class

the others stare curiously
murmuring indistinct things

but the truth was out
already i knew
the definitive constants:
Hugo, Baudelaire
Rimbaud, Verlaine, Lamartine

my teachers had accepted
me in their circle.

a meek attempt

the only insanity
i ever found in people:
false preaching well wrought
in their circuitry
trampling all tangible facts

like an avalanche of snow
forming and getting bigger
encapsulating their brains

to war they answer: justice!
to famine they say: mercy!
to death they say: salvation!

and the generic answer
floating above them
flashing in bright neon lights

RESUSCITATION

the erasure of malice
the undoing of error
the second chance at living
after having lived

those of us worth saving left
this place long a-go;
and those of you who came here
to read my stuff ho-ping to
be saved know it is too late.

Three

Isn't that, after all, the purpose of art? To refine our voices until they hit the right tone?

Letter to Poetry magazine

Dear Editors,

I have been a fan of Poetry since I first started to write. It's no secret that the magazine is coveted by newcomers and experts alike in the field, yet for me it has been a story of unrequited love. Every rejection has been a vibrant stimulant for me to pursue and understand this art further, and to latch on to it deeper. Just recently I had experienced some sort of artistic crisis where I couldn't find my voice anymore in anything I wrote. Or rather, I recognized my voice was not my voice but more of a spillage that needed refinement. Isn't that, after all, the purpose of art? To refine our voices until they hit the right tone?

I am sending some of my newer work to be considered. It would be great to have any of them featured in the upcoming edition of the magazine. The poetry is a set of experimental variations loosely based on the original haiku form. I have tried to add structure to my previously messy verses by retaining the 5- and 7- metrics all while playing with the overall form to set it free.

Thank you for your time and consideration. I look forward to hearing from you.

Ever yours

On Paris

*P*aris is E.E Cummings talking about courage. Paris is the sidewalk cafes, the bums and hippies and drunks sitting there discussing the new generation, the world's demise, the secret doors that lead to heaven...

Paris is also the black woman carrying her children in each arm, along with a third in a stroller on the train. Paris is the Chinese and the Japanese students crowding university courts, the cheap Thai place next to the Algerian or Turkish fast food stop at every street corner.

Paris is the place we return to after being smashed into oblivion, it is the cigarette smoke of the artists and the writers and the savants. But it is also the place of the non-artists, the suppressors of great literature and great paintings and great works, the anti-cultural skateboarders and bike riders and mobsters filling the streets in riot or ganging up in front of parliament walls.

Picasso got a street and a museum named after him here, Van Gogh would revel in the Starry Night exhibit flashing in all colors in projected lights off a raw mural. Hemingway and Faulkner would sit and applaud while sipping their black coffee, joined by Hugo still mourning the death of his daughter and liberty. The French get agitated when they hear Arabs speaking freely next to them; they think it's taunting or provocative to them. The other Europeans still try to measure up their roots to make sure they make the cut, unsure whether to be at ease or be wary of the passive aggressiveness teeing up in the atmosphere.

From my window I can spot French police surveying the neighborhood, carrying tear gas and guns and bats in their pockets. They too have forgotten the meaning of freedom of values, and they forget what they are defending. But what is there left to fight for? The poor blacks coming in from Africa, imported daily to consume more resources? Or the arabs feeding off scarce produce, profiting from the country's generous givings in food and healthcare instead of a Frenchman who'd happily walk down and get his unemployment check?

France is the new America and paris, los angeles: smog, grim, grey, a little heavy on the eyes.

As I write this, I still think of the life I have here: I have been able to settle with virtually nothing to start with. No food, no money, no car. And as it is often the case when you move into a new country or start a new foundation (in most cases bare), you tend to forget these problematic key stones you are missing and ignore them completely. At one time, carrying a few euros in my pocket, I thought I was broke to the bone and without any money at all. The result: I starved myself for 3 days and 2 nights before hearing the clanging of the coins in my pants while getting dressed. Now for a normal person this idea of depriving yourself entirely of something would pose a lot of problems and would certainly render moving to a new country more complex. But when you are a writer you just take it in and consider it to be food for the page. Sooner than later your lips dry out from lack of food and water and before you know it you're scratching your limbs because you stopped showering. That's the major force of any writer, as I always say: endurance. They are receptive to pain and deprivation and forbiddance. Their painkillers are much more effective than those of a normal person and they fire much more actively (some would even say non-stop).

Anyhow, I managed to avoid a large chunk of the population since arriving here, and I hope to keep the ball going in that direction. Paris hasn't helped my faith much (although I have seen a large number of churches and cathedrals) but if I could, I would even go as far as praying for things to stay this way. I have moved from being a recluse curled up in a small part of the world to being a recluse curled up in a slightly bigger part of it. From the moment I landed here I could sense the culture and the music and the free-spirited minds floating all about, and I rushed into the small room I rented and threw my suitcase about. Now it is somewhere, possibly half-open with most of the items scattered, but I don't care, hehe, I don't care about traveling or all of

Europe opening up to me now or invoking the great minds that grazed this beautiful city or were toucher or moved by it. I am looking straight into the light, flashing at me from old vintage manufactured cars, swooping through the diners and hopping from one streetlamp to another.

There is a blue horizon here stretching much farther than the biggest river, coursing faster than the row boats and the cruise ships which makes you want to pull up a towel and wrap it over your body and pour a glass of wine after a long, hot shower.

mix variety

i don't know
what it is
that makes Parisian nights
both quiet
and agitated
here I sit
at the outskirts of this city
lights blazing towards the sky
like pillars of drawn paintbrushes
fuming into the glazing skyline
meanwhile here my floorplan
is flattened out by harps
laid like dead bodies
chords overlaid on top
and across each other
i tiptoe
like walking in a minefield
turning the piano music loud
to cover the detonations
and make it to the phone

my friend
wants me to meet
his new girlfriend
whom he promised
to introduce

to the Poet
no, no
i say,
not now
not today.

and is it true
that windless skies
are a sign of love?

two bodyguards
out there waiting
to take me in the patrol
jeep
they want to grab me
by the arms
and clobber me
at the back of the vehicle
knock me out cold
for obscene and provocative
writing
you better clean up
your act, son,
one of them says
or else you'll be missing
a few fingers the next time
you type!

but hey,
i wasn't afraid

of delayed war
(hell, they've been
talking about one
right around the corner
for a few weeks now)
molotov bombs
putin in front of the Russians
promising salvation
more speeches by America
all talk and no deliverables
who the hell is
supervising all of this
anyhow?

and onto other matters
now I discover
they are teaching writing
they have seminars
and everything
you can even
major in it
and get licensed
to write.
that's not all
you can also
specialize
in a form of writing
yeah,
they're now

deconstructing
it
as if
the rabid theories
around abstract
categorical grammars
weren't enough
for us to recover
from…
what were
they doing
to the language
what were they doing
promising folks
they could become masters
and doctors in poetry
fiction
journal-entry writing
playwriting
they've officially soaked
up all the talent
squeezed the juice
out of it
and drank it

allah! allah!
our brothers in the east
are shouting
god! god!

replies the west,
what difference
did it make?
you might as well
call him Judas
he'll only answer
when and if
he feels like it
and maybe
there was a reason
all these populations
were deprived
of the higher force

maybe
we have been immunized
against the horrible atrocities
we are responsible for
and we are all
riding in a carriage
with no driver
heading for the edge
of the hillside…
flyers don't fly
no more
walkers don't walk
and poetry writers
kill with words
and blame it on

knives and blades
thieves are being pounded
and robbed
politicians erected
into statues
with rosaries around
their necks
angry mobs
marching toward their demise
burning books
art directors
assembled
in the screen room
planning the next blockbuster
to keep brainwashing
the minds

all this
through the lens of raindrops
against my Parisian window
little slits of truth
dropping off and amassing on my pane
like puddled mirrors

tomorrow I have a plane
to catch
to salvage a country
that can't be saved
where all the 20-year-old
girls

are getting married
to 30-year-old
guys
and the 40-year-old
men
are trying to seduce
the 20-year-old
girls
and the gas strike
and the bread and wheat strike
and the electricity strike
and the water strike
ah, paris!
save me!
hold me tight in your arms
and never let me go!

Apocalypse fire

giant hands
rising from podium
spelling pandemonium
wild tigers
leaping through
rings of fire
i have seen men in suits
cut themselves over torn
dollar bills
drowning
jumping off bridges
holding off artificial
constructed paradises
for a little more ransom

those who are portrayed
with heads covered in bags
on the guillotine
are never the ones who
have earned their place there

we have reached a point of
no return
where some of us
unwillingly
unconditionally

take the fall for
the misgivings and mishaps
of others

never mind the preaching
of the Greek philosophers
aristotle and plato are dead
nietzsche is laughed at
and recycled badly
barely chewed and
spit out in some
reject low-key vomit
projectile version
while the chorus sings
for hitler
invoking and praising genocides
hoping for the return of adolf

cousin squirrels hide in tree
peep holes
alerting mother nature of
the greatest danger since
mass forest fires
split mass popular opinion
spreading like wild bush
and black thorns

the great armies of the past
would have plummeted
and fallen at their face

swatted like house flies
resting still on every side cup
in every home in Beirut
while Paris sings for Christmas
and New York city chants
"down the emperor
down the ruler"

meanwhile the Japanese
are calling for the great
godzilla to save them
and swallow half the globe
bringing visions of Dante's
poem
the poet revolutionary who
had to write about his soul burning
in many hells
languishing to the end
before reaching salvation
and touching ultimate
and final truth
which I am convinced
more and more
does not belong
to this world.

Written on the night of the revolution

- I -
very very bullish
i come out with my strophes
and stanzas
and verses
like a wild religious mongrel
protesting in the streets
a revolutionary holding
arms and banners
in the name of
the army of god
black blue serpentine flags
soaring to the sky
i come at you with
rhythm
poem
smoke
and gun barrels
with invisible eyes that
have survived the desert storm
a masked face
that never yields
palms heavy with
gun powder

- II -
they will know fear
they will know what it's
like
to thwart partisans banging
at them
from the other end
where the phoenix and the
bald eagle roost together
ravaged neighborhoods
where kids once assembled
and kicked an old deflated
soccer ball
under hanging clotheslines
on abandoned balconies
leading to obscure corridors
housing flashing television screens
like diodes
bursting with guns and sound
and image and firearms
disclaiming the people of
the revolution
fighting for corruption
taking a stand
with blood-thirsty
soul-thirsty
leaders

- III -

in the name of the father
the holy-blessed father
the pious son jesus
christ bless thy name
walking bare on foul shores
defunct land
and the holy spirit
the holy ghost floating
rising above the heads
of steinbeck
miller
turgenev
faulkner
old-man hemingway
opium burroughs
gay ginsberg
rowdy kerouac
plouc, plouc, plouc…

- IV -

ladies scream in horror
shed tears of cruel sorrow
they sleep naked under
unwashed covers
while the land of the free
outside is busy
huddling
calling them out

for liberty
aligning hope, faith,
prosperity
in a never-seen-before
scene of epiphany
rise, rise
my quiet people
the sage
the erudite
the blasphemous
the outlaw
the exiled
they have banished us
and locked us in the history
books
recorded our cries of mercy
stirred and embroiled us in false cacophony

- V -
but like the holy communion
we have infiltrated their
temples
and we are here
firm, true, brimming
with no fear.

An open essay to this generation's rising writers

Okay. You know, I've seen lately a strange surge in writers publishing books. People claiming they have instantly become writers and launched themselves on the scene. It's like the new hip thing to do now, in 2019, like weed or listening to heavy metal bands or wearing spike bracelets.

It's the trend.

I read those news, and I can't help but feel bothered. I get nausea for several days. I get an unshakable stomach ache that won't go away for weeks. I feel numb in my limbs. These self-proclaimed "new writers", where did they come from? Where were they hiding when the real ones were busy getting the word out and diffusing it? It seems right now that anyone can write a book effortlessly, and more alarmingly, thoughtlessly.

Well, let me tell you something. The people I've read, people like Anderson, Bradbury, Carver, Dostoevsky, they all were prolific. And some of them even happened to write books during the same time or era. That's not the issue here. But all of them—without exception—had a thought process behind it. And by it, I don't just mean the books they published. I mean the process. The writing. The writer. The wordform as a whole.

Who of the newcomers can claim to have that? Surely not the up-and-coming hip and trendy young adult writing her first diary-turned-into-book. Or the shy college guy who's just published his "thoughts" in verse and called them a poetry collection.

But wait, you'll tell me, shouldn't we be encouraging writers? Aren't you the one always crying out for the lack of writing, literature, art?

Yes, but these people are hurting the art form. These people give a bad name and a bad rep for the good writers and poets of the world. You see, by allowing themselves to let books like these come out, they are degrading the good books on the market. How do you expect a new reader, or a curious person eager to pick up a new book, to be able to tell the difference between a good one and a piece of shit? It's not their responsibility, and we certainly can't hold them accountable for it. Rather, it's our responsibility as poets and writers to ensure we put the best books out there on the market for the audience.

But now, now the market's flooded with trash and false labels. I see the word "novel" stapled on nearly every manuscript:

> "*A coming-of-age story of a young girl into womanhood. [Insert author's name]'s first novel!*"
>
> "*A story that unveils the workings of depression on the human mind. A fantastic novel.*"
>
> "*A novel on the shift in power of the different political parties and their change in stance.*"

Frankly, it's ridiculous. And this is coming from a guy who's never been true to form or adhered to a strict shape in writing.

So what do you want, you ask me? Well, that's a damn good question.

What do I want?

Surely not to bring back the great writers. Surely not more of Tolstoy, Rilke, Wordsworth, Shakespeare, Byron. Surely not Nietzsche. Surely not Shelley or Plath. But I want respect. Respect for the ones who have taken up that calling and have made it their creed.

Writing is not about making books. It's not about being backed by gay-rights activist publishers or feminist publishing houses. Books were never and will never be the end product of writing. Neither is the writer.

The job of the writer has always been and will always be to live by the word. And that might mean a series of things: to abstain from eating, to drink excessively, to refrain from smoking, to avoid the bus or public commute, to curse in traffic, to shower in cold water only. Etcetera, etcetera.

Now if a person's lucky, they might get out a book of all those things listed above. And if they push their luck, then they might just get to be called a writer. But for that, you would need to lick the pot of gold extended by the hands of the gods smiling at your little squirming from side to side in your little one-room apartment, watching you helplessly battle the cold weather in Europe with no heating. It could also mean total isolation, being forgotten, pushing back anyone knocking at your door, not answering your calls, and living off hard bread and corn flakes for a number of months.

There. That's how you form a thought process. That's how you allow yourself to absorb the aura sphere that is art. That's how you make it into the history books and seal your name in the great works of literature.

Now enough about this. There is an unfinished paper manuscript that needs dusting, contemplation, and completion. It's going to be a novel.

On disturbing the peace

sometimes it's good to stay away
take a break from the machine
un-wind
leave the word at peace
just get away from it
for a while
trying to connect
art and life
constantly
is tiring
writing
is identity
but it's also pain
submission
obedience to the word
and that can get to your head
and that can get to be
too much
sometimes…
so yes
yes
writing
is of essence
for a writer
and without it
he is naked

and empty
but there are times where
he needs to take off his cape
and breathe ordinary air
fuh fuh fuh
and sink back into life
and there
there he realizes
that the washed-out French songs
playing on the French Riviera
and the water you drink from the sink
and the alleys that made Faulkner and Hemingway
and Anderson
keep boxing the individual
seeking to break free
and nobody
gets to be anybody other than
what others want them to be
they run around fulfilling
other people's dreams and needs
like obligations
even the artists
now look to strengthen their connections
they're as dirty as politicians
sneaky
stubborn
hypocritical
and the publishers
and the magazines

publish this or that individual
based on name or title
or face
no themes
no content
and the voices still look for an out
they get shut out by the day
in little towns and small neighborhoods
or on graffiti and sticker walls
on the edge of big cities
the sky touches the ground
kisses my face
and darkens with wind and rain and fireballs
and the word in its little corner by the bed
whispers to me
and the predators in my closet rumble
and rattle restlessly
calling for me, their
savior
no more French songs
no more train station announcements
no more billboards, please
no more European cities
no more pushing my mind
and stretching its limits
no more drinking tea
while Aznavour mourns Amsterdam
in the background
no more fangirls,

no more readers, please
the racket won't stop
i've got cold feet
god is preaching the bible again
the pitchforks are raised downtown
the sky is pale purple
and nobody knows why.

Writing about writing

writing about writing
is boring;
einstein was wrong;
the universe
doesn't expand
it shrinks;
and we dissolve in it
bit by bit;
what matters
is what we leave behind;
the trail
is it substantial?
is it holy?
is it real?

Lenny

when I was in high school
my friend Lenny and i
dreamed of becoming poets.
we wrote lines
on little scraps of paper
in class
and read them to each other
every night.

i used to call him
on the landline
and lock my bedroom door
and read with him
for hours
before my poor mother
came in screaming on me
and banging
bang bang bang
for me to open up:
"get off the phone!
you're making the bill RUN TOO HIGH!"
ah, mother,
you wouldn't understand,
i'd think inside my high school brain
we're past being men,
we are poets.

we honored Baudelaire,
Verlaine,
Rimbaud,
Lamartine
we wrote for them
and we impersonated them.
"that's good,"
Lenny would say,
"read that line to me again,"
in reference
to one of the poems i wrote.
"someday," he said,
"someday we'll both become
poets! renegades of society!
heroes! madmen!"
"YES!" i screamed
"YES! YES!" like a madman.

today i am putting down the line
cautiously
aware that the path
i've undertaken
is far too risky
and far from being
safe and sure
while Lenny
is being rushed in and out
of hospitals.

they have me prosecuted

for the words i lay down for them
and old Lenny
well, they got him in
for substance abuse
he's been riding drugs
for almost his entire life now
and some nights i can feel him
i can hear his distorted voice
distant and weak
wondering where it all went wrong
and downhill for him
wondering how the wasted years
caught up to his talent
and deprived him of his truth
our truth

he carries his weight in pills
and i carry mine
in words
and it is much
too heavy
for us

let's just say
we are both fighting battles
we can't win.

Stems from the edge of silence

i sit here
and play with the ball of life
fresh off the back
of another book release
but something is still there
something is eating up at me
chewing on the back of my brains
is it the word?
even getting it all out
and watching it take book-form
was not enough
to be rid of it

people talk about
talent
but all it is in fact
is an aberration
a total disembodiment
of mind and soul.

it is an untreatable
illness
uncurable
cancer
pure cancer
that keeps biting bits

and pieces
of me
while i slowly disassemble
into the incoming gust
from my porch.

i watch it take me
i watch it triumph
and slowly erase my name
and bury it into the ground
sink it deep down
into the magma-laden pits of the earth.

today it is me
tomorrow it is another
who will bear token
and be selected
as the next sacrificial lamb
to the word.

meanwhile the sun still rises
the stadiums still pack themselves
with football enthusiasts
the cheerleaders cheer on
in high school basketball games
the jocks chew their gum
and hit game-winning shots
and the donkeys push back the farmers
on the hill

refusing the climb of life
refusing the clutter and the weight
and the forceful push and the power shift
and the poet sits
standstill
waiting for the storm of the word
to take over
the living and the dead.

The piano man

He sat in one of the corners of a local bookstore in Paris. He wasn't a main attraction—the people in the area much preferred trying out new food than listening to some old retired man bashing his fingers against the piano keys.

Strange, it was. The people, the damn people. They had their priorities all wrong in a city that offered them so much art and culture and soul. In all fairness, though, the piano man never expected a crowd to show up when he played.

He wore the same outfit every Sunday afternoon when he performed: a black tuxedo and a black sharp hat from which the few greying hairs on the side of his head popped out like little white strings. His sharp attire was much more in veneration of his art than his audience—he worshiped the piano and its keys and its frame touching down the ancient library carpet.

I went to see him with my girlfriend. We had wandered into that library by mistake on a rainy day. But then again, we were both melancholic with life and plain fed up with existence. We drank the sadness of the human race in our coffee cups and postulated questions about the meaning of it all. No matter how much we tried, we couldn't find the answer to that.

So we discovered the piano man, sitting next to a wall of books shelved in order like soldiers in an army line. He was hammering his fingers against the keys, biting his lips occasionally and closing his eyes for the most part of the show. I always like to think he handled the piano the way he would fiddle with a woman: gently stroking it, leaning in from time to time to whisper to it, flashing smiles and even winking at it while he played. The people gathered, they always gathered when they saw their numbers flocked in a certain area. We were among them, witnessing a musical genius at work.

The angels and the gods were summoned that afternoon. The roaring thunder outside was silenced. The piano man became a magician and the library his stage. He had us all in his bag of tricks.

The keys were ringing, orgasming to the caresses of his fingers, roaring at times, hushing at others, resting, screaming, prowling, singing, chiming. The prodigy himself was tingling and the rest of us were in awe.

I looked at my girl. She was breathtaking, despite her ongoing struggles with the human race. She let herself go in the music, just listening, observing, listening again, humming parts of the melody that kept climbing and crashing back down, peaking and resonating, oscillating and saturating in her, me, us. I caught her hand vibrating in the air, as if it had detached from the rest of her body and was in a state of free-fall. The motion that carried it came from the music, or the wind, or the outside downpour, or her inner conviction in the power of the scene.

I, being generally a tasteless and distrusting man, defiant and wary of other humans by default, couldn't keep it in me to hold my joy. I couldn't refrain my lips from parting and exhibiting a wide smile that painted itself across my face like a badly-drawn straight line.

In the back some folks were helping themselves to some sly comments. A connoisseur was being critical to the style of music played, another was asking about the piano man's name and credentials while another one was just making noise. In the end, they all were.

There was no room for dialogue, but the piano man took the time to grace the crowd with his charming looks, hopping from one member to the next with his sagged old eyes, carrying the hope for humanity inside of them, like some kind of modern-day Sisyphus the world had been oblivious to. He carried on, and I grabbed my girlfriend's hand and caught some of her vibrations.

Listening to music in a library was a new form of exultation. It evoked memories of Bach, Chopin, Beethoven, Stravinsky, Liszt. They were all present that day, all there, and it was one of the rare times where I didn't need a drink to be able to summon them. They played with the piano man, ardently, each to their own wavelength, and in turn we were treated to a real feast.

Our ears were being stuffed with musicality, and the melancholy that had haunted me for so many sleepless nights was slowly creeping out of my system.

I looked at my girl.

'hey,' she said with her eyes.

'hey,' I said.

I was never good with the small talk.

She gripped my hand firmer, forever, and I submitted to the cult. The music, free and intact, still gathered followers. Communication dissolved. Words drowned. The library offered us pure emotions, emotions you read about in the great books of poetry or the epochs of legends.

When he was done playing, the piano man got up, supported by one of the piano legs, and hoisted his hand up like a racing champion. The crowd applauded hard. Most of them cheered and made weird noises that broke the sacred silence of the bookstore. My girlfriend stood in place, drunk with music, drunk with emotion and pleasure and sensation, overwhelmed by the act that had been delivered in front of her. I looked at her and thought about how different the next time drinking coffee together would be.

The piano man made a swift exit through the crowd and vanished. He had garnered a following, but he had given them solace in return. Solace in knowing the rain wouldn't wash away their pain and worries, but wouldn't drown them or hurt them either.

For me, it was clarity about the things that still had meaning for me in life—things people were quick to diminish every time I talked about them—like music, peace, silence, talent. That belief was renewed and reinforced in me. I walked out of the store still grabbing onto my girlfriend's hand. I took a look at the nearby bars to try to spot the piano man there. I suspected he would need a drink after a cathartic performance like that.

The bars in the area had no indoor seating and offered little space, so it was easy to search for people hanging in one of them. But the piano man was nowhere in sight. I guess not all artists relied on drinking to produce.

On the walk back the rain had stopped. A bright moon was seen distributing its little light across the boulevard. My girlfriend pointed at it and said, 'this is beautiful'.

I nodded. It was one of the rare things that still were.

Another me

'do you want another drink?'
'yeah, yeah, pour me another one!'
I get up and get the bottle.
'you've been drinking all night,' I say. 'don't you ever stop?'
'I stop when I reach my limit,' he says.
'when's that?'
'I'll let you know when I get there.'
He had the crazy eyes, the crazy bulging red eyes, the eyes of a demon.
'why don't I see you around during the day?' I ask.
'I don't get out much during the day.'
'why's that? not a fan of sunlight?'
'not particularly.'
He takes off his jacket and throws it on the other side of the divan. I notice a big red stain on it.
'what's that?'
He chuckles. 'oh, that?' he says with a nasty grin. 'that's someone's blood. I saw a man killing a youngster for his pocket money the other night in a back-alley. I watched the whole thing. It was like the movies: a lot of screaming, struggling, threatening,

grappling, knifing, gunk shots of blood splattering everywhere.'
'and you watched the whole thing?'
'hell yeah! I got a real kick out of it! You can't ask for much better action during the night unless you're copulating with a fine female. Oh, to rip her skin apart, to tear her in half! Yeah, baby!'
'you're psychotic.'
'hell, yeah, baby!'
'you're demented!'
'pour me more liquor!'
I get up and get another bottle.
'aren't you drinking with me?' he asks.
'I'm at my limit.'
'you're not a very pleasant character.'
'you aren't very pleasant either.'
'I'll kill you! I swear I'll kill you!'
'you can't kill me. The night's almost over. The sun's about to get up.'
'why doesn't the sun just give up? Why does it keep trying?'
'maybe it's trying to keep the balance between us guys and you guys.'
'bullshit!'
He gets up, fetches his jacket, puts it on, raises the collar. 'where's my guitar?' he shouts.
'you don't have a guitar.'

'damn it, where are my car keys?'
'you don't have a car.'
'bullshit! I have a 2-seater! A sportscar! fresh out of the garage with a new paint job!'
'maybe you put it next to the guitar,' I suggest.
'fuck you!' he says. he storms out.
the house sinks in a strange quiet. through the blinds the first rays of sunlight start to creep in. the next-door neighbor's hens begin to cluck, cluck cluck cluck, left and right, right and left, I see them shoving each other in that small garden. I even smell them.
I grab my car keys from the counter and go out to the driveway. I unlock the car—wary of not leaving any key scratches on the new paint job—and take out my jacket. I go back inside and look at the red stain on the sleeve. I throw the jacket in the washer. back in the main room, I pull out a new bottle of liquor and sit on the couch. I pour myself a drink, looking at the sun, at the room, the sound of the washer beating against my mind, as the black-coated guitar lay in the corner.

On writing

writing had
no beginnings
or happy endings;
it was all
middles
littered with
long pauses
in between.

To Jeff

Dear J.D.,
It might be too early
For this letter
But what the heck –
Life's too short
To figure out the right timing
To say what we want to say

Anyway,
What I wanted to say
Is that I am glad
You are now my publisher
Seriously
You and me
We found each other
In the purest hazard
And instantly clicked
Like a matchstick
And a flame
We made a combustible fire –
No, a cannonball
That exploded
All over the literary scene.
I'm not saying
We're the greatest team
Out there

But I honestly think
We can give
The best of them
A good run
For their money.

From the time we met
You cupped your hands
Around my work
And treated it
As your own –
You've dealt
With my hysterical
Psyche
Without fear
Or prior warning

And yeah
It hasn't been long enough yet
But I feel it
I foresee it
I can see this partnership stretching out
Into the wind
Into the vast forests
Sprouting endless trees
Spearing high into the skyline

We've already come good
And made a couple of good books
Together:

I am happy
With the poetry volume
And even more with
My second novel!

Well,
I guess most of what I have to tell
You already know
I will keep pushing down the words
For as long as I can
That is a vow
I never hope to break
And I know you will do
Everything
To make them come alive
In some form
Book, manuscript, letter
Sculpture, painting, film
Whatever it is
I don't believe
I can trust anyone
With the madness of myself
Like I trust you
And so
Here's to more
To many more works together
10, 20, 100, 100 000
And by the way
I might have a new batch

Coming up soon
(Poetry it looks like it's turning out)
But we can discuss that
Another time

And so
Here's to you
And your work
And this journey
Hoping for more
And getting a kick
And a rush of blood to the face
Out of every second of it.

Yours truly

Fearing the blues

It was night and we were both feeling sick. I had the running nose, the sore throat, the coughs. Diane was breathing heavily and coughing notoriously.

We crawled into bed early that night.

'Don't you want to write?' she asked me.

'Not tonight,' I said. 'I'm stuck.'

'Stuck on what?'

'Stuck on a title. I can't find a title for my damn piece.'

That piece had been written almost a week now. It was nearing expiration. A piece without a title never looked good to me. It felt unfinished, incomplete. Blemished. I wanted to pin a header on that thing and relegate it to the drawer with the rest of my stuff. Diane was calling for patience.

It was raining outside. I watched the droplets of water smash against the balcony floor.

'It's a bad night,' I said.

'Why's that?'

'It's a sad night.'

Diane was still coughing excessively. 'Fuck,' she said.

'Fuck,' I said.

She got out of bed and sat on the edge. She lit a cigarette and started smoking.

I watched her. I watched her and thought about that nasty cough, about my blues, about the failed writing, about my sickness with life.

Tomorrow it will rain, the evening news had declared. We needed groceries for the house. We needed detergent for the bathroom. We needed to clean the place up because Diane was expecting people over. I needed to do my laundry.

'Fuck,' I said.

'What's the matter, baby,' Diane asked, finishing up her cigarette. She pressed it against the ashtray, half-lit, half-finished. She would come back for it later. That was her idea of mitigating smoking.

I wished I had that kind of commitment. I could never put down a drink before it was fully finished. My mind saw it more of a challenge and set the gauntlet for my body.

Diane didn't like it when I drank. It annoyed her that something other than writing could captivate me and trap me that much. 'It's going to be the end of you,' she said to me. Every time.

What's going to be the end of me is this title. This title that never came. It was trapped somewhere, and no matter how much I dig and dig, I can't reach it.

Diane came back to bed. I know she worries about me. About how demented I get with writing when it doesn't go my way.

I worry about her too. I worry about that cough that won't go away. I worry the rain won't stop and we'll never get out of the house again. I worry Paris won't smell or feel the same again.

I worry about going somewhere. Or not going anyplace at all. I liked it here. It was eerily quiet and hurried and bustled at the same time.

There was not much traffic in the suburbs, but a lot of people. Especially people walking their dogs. Dogs that didn't have the energy to bark, but were just content with walking. Just like artists weren't making art, just content with hanging out in the streets and public places.

The rain was still going. Diane was still coughing. I still had the running nose and the life blues.

Diane turned to the side and faced me. 'It will rain tomorrow,' she said.

'Yeah, I know,' I said.

'We might not be able to get out of the house.'

'Yeah.'

'What if the rain doesn't stop and we can't ever go out again?'

I leaned in and kissed her. 'If the dogs can make it without barking, we'll be alright,' I told her.

Then I got up, closed the shades and put my untitled piece in the drawer.

Clogs

A rat comes up to me. He is gray-haired, gray-whiskered, gray-bearded.

I am in my dark room. The bed is shifting, sliding into darkness.

The rat comes up to me. His squeaky voice whispers in my ear that the sink is clogged.

I nod at him. Uh-huh. The sink has been clogged for the past three months and a cesspool of filth and food residue is now swimming in it.

There's more, the rat keeps squeaking, spitting out hair and dust balls from his tiny mouth. He tells me that the shower and bathroom drains are clogged too.

They have been for months. The water had overflown and the drains were spouting liquid like fountains. It was nearly impossible to walk in there. Only I'd forgotten about it.

I got up and paced the room. I stared at the square floor, the little cuts in the ceiling and the cracks in the walls. I remembered walking into the apartment on the first day with my landlady screaming over my shoulder: RENT IS DUE ON THE 7TH OF THE MONTH. DON'T BE LATE. I never was since then.

I distinctly remember a beam of sunlight perusing the room on that day. Now shades of dark groom me in my sleep, in my wake, in my existence in this place. The shadows make for good company when you are alone: they constantly remind you they are there, they are present, they are watching.

I hear footsteps upstairs. Is it a plumber, finally coming in to put me out of my misery? It was hard to have your life depend on someone else's job.

Everything was coming to me now: the rat squeaking, the water gurgling, the landlady screaming and harassing people at the reception desk, the plumber that might or might not come, the faltering pipeline behind my walls, the rusty sewage system implemented beneath my floor.

Walking in filth put a man in touch with reality it brought him closer than making his own ham and cheese sandwich and eating it in the cold with no heating in Parisian wintry weather, it brought him closer than hand-washing clothes when the washer was out, it brought him closer than killing the deathly spider and leaving it there to dissolve on the floor because there was nothing to pick it up with.

The rat scurries now, he goes back to his small hole (that I hadn't noticed until now) in my wall to join his other rat friends and possibly tell them about what he saw in the bigger world. I thought how much tidier his hole would look than my room, and if I could possibly visit it someday or live in it for a while.

I cracked open my window, just small enough to ensure no creature would crawl or fly or fit into it. The natural world was much more organized and lively than mine.

I looked over at the lyrics books stacked on my bed. The songs I'd written over the years were no closer to saving me than that no-show plumber.

I have been playing the guitar and performing everywhere for the past twenty years. The people who listened to my music told me it transported them to other worlds. Now I want to slit open this dimension and move away from it all: the performances that don't seem real, the music that doesn't seem real, the lyrics that don't seem real. Hell, even this room doesn't seem real. Everything is sliding sideways, and I am the fairy-killer hell-raising captain steering this sinking ship.

In the distance a dog is barking. I could seldom hear women screaming out my name in an almost unified chant. Now it is just the dog and he sounds much more pleased than me with the way life is shaping up ahead.

Another pounding against my ceiling. There is definitely movement upstairs but it doesn't interest me. It doesn't even stir me or trouble me anymore.

I open my side-closet and check for my guitar. A black mid-range Cort G350 series with a vinyl flame glazing the body. I don't feel like touching it, I am ashamed to touch it, just prefer to leave it there.

Leave it in the shade of the wreckage surrounding it, leave a separation between it and the rest of the room.

In the bathroom the water keeps going, and it is strange how much more powerful of a sound it makes now, how acutely it is heard. Maybe it was me thinking about it so much, thinking about stepping in shit the next time I wanted to shower.

I should have been a circus clown. I wouldn't lose out on the thrill of performing and entertaining crowds while being provided a decent room and some warm food to live by. My only handicap would be lucking in with women, but they have been scarce even in this life.

Having a woman here now would have certainly made things easier. It would have split the pain if anything. She could have been smoking a cigarette sitting half-naked on my bed with the rest of her clothes laying all about the room, dusting off the tip of her smoke on my floor and scattering the ashes on my dishes. That would still have been good for me.

A restless quiet sets in. The music of the gurgling water fades, the pumping of the water reservoir heater dissipates and the tapping of the clogging pipes behind my walls recedes.

The shadows are gone, I don't feel them anymore. They've disappeared entirely and pulled out of this toxic atmosphere. I no longer heard the whiskers of the rat fretting and rubbing off whenever he spoke. I no longer heard the music of my own compositions.

The only thing I heard was the dog still barking at a distance.

Live it

the sunlight crashed
against my full body
binding me
to the earth

i felt it
i felt it
for the first time

sometimes
a man
has to fight
so hard
for life
that he forgets
to live it.

Four

I have read all the love poems of the world

Ecosystem

you could tell
from this city
that the people here
needed love
and
togetherness
more than
anywhere
else.

Survival

in the crowd
i am always
the one
who is not
picked out:
the others
highlight
themselves
and shine
spotlights
above their heads.
they think
they have it
all figured out;
they don't.
the stray cats
and the rodents
in the streets
know how to
survive
much better
than us.

I've read all the love poems of the world

those that talk about
enjoying a book with music on
most of them are about a woman
some of them are about many women
they have worn down the language
with the use of expansive vocabulary
and vivid imagery

i have read all the love poems of the world
i have been beaten to the line by some

other poet every time
and intoxicated with
the silence that comes with
running out of words

there is nothing left to write
all the lines spoken out
and read before bedtime
in dim lamplight
the last love word exhausted,
consumed
swallowed
shot out of the throat
into the feather pillow

there is nothing left for me to write
i have run out of line space
the margins have fallen off the pages
and the dotted blank gaps erased
i go berserk
berserk scratching the top of my head
smoking my cigarette in puffs
making smoke circles
looking half-mad, half-desperate
trying to stay agile but falling behind on pace
i cannot keep up
with the amount of love poems sinking the earth
making rooms, caves, entire lore on the history of love

there are no more words
and the words I cannot write
already belong
to you.

active function

he drew a large bubble
on the blackboard
chalked a few arrows
incoming
and outgoing
from it

to demonstrate
the trigger
from which stemmed
the principle
of artificial intelligence

i found myself
bizarrely attending
that class
among future geniuses
of the nation
advocates
of the AI empire
that will sweep our jobs
and eliminate
our contributions

i heard the professor
(he was most probably
a doctor in the matter)

prophesize
that most of us
will lose our current professions
to sentient high-powered machines

and proceed
to list
some of these
'lost' professions
among which
came up mine

oh well,
i thought
walking out
of the class

at least
they cannot strip me
of my other function
being a drinker

and reported
nevertheless
to the somber desk
where my work
was still waiting
for me
for the night at least

i refilled the printer
with A4 paper
slumped
in front of
the typer

and started
writing.

Chicago

trying to ship
another one
of my poems
overseas
to *Poetry Magazine*
while a poetess
in Detroit, Michigan
has a crown of sonnets
accepted
for the February 2020 edition
while the senate
is running rings
around the angry mob
while my girlfriend
sleeps solemnly
under the sheets.
i promised to make
love to her
tonight
but well,
that's another
failed thing
besides this poem
and the one
i am going to send
to Poetry.

i've lost
the ability
to count days
to read and use
calendars
to perform
20 straight sit-ups
to last through
an entire basketball game
to function properly
in a social milieu.
well outside
the carolers
are preparing their cheers
and soon the snow will cover
the driveway
like a carpet
and I'll have to get the shovel
ready
and the house will be submerged
with presents and wrapping paper
destined for relatives
we seldom speak to.

but that's what my girlfriend
worries about
as for me,
i just worry
about making the coffee

cooking steak
every other Sunday
and this poem.

well,
not so much this poem
anymore
or the one
on its way
just now
to Chicago, Illinois.

Birdstorm

nicotine addiction
herbal infusions
on top of piano playing
hands to nowhere
touching my face
like a great and wonderous
jehovah
we could have meant
something more
her whispers keep tracking
me into small alleyways
i look at vomit stains
on the bathroom stall
a purple toothbrush
to eternity
and remember
catching a plane
with her
at Orly airport
amid disrupted talks
of sex fantasies
and crisis
taking long strolls
in the Bois de Boulogne
thinking
Paris has never been

this good to us
and that individuals
of good heart and good faith
deserved a shot at real happiness

now dishpans covered
with her fingermarks
lonely songless nights
are the blueprint of my forthcoming
days

mad with silence
mad with poetry
mad with endless books
sweaters
sweatshirts
jackets
socks
unwearable
meaningless Quran
meaningless Bible
meaningless Cantos

she is gone
and so is everything
with her.

This woman

this woman tells me
i do not know
how to love;
and, in bed,
she tells me
i am the greatest lover
of all-time.
i shack with her
in a little sun-covered room
with a glass-door
to a balcony:
we've smeared the room
and the balcony
with tear-blood memories
and when the last butterfly has taken off
and flown off one of the walls
she starts to threaten me
with a frying pan
raised up to my cheeks;
i threaten
to kill her
and walk away
in cold-blood.
but you see,
it's all safe,
it's as safe

as lighting a candle:
the moment you hold the fiery matchstick
and watch it get eaten up by the flame
you worry you will not make it
but you light the candle
and the flame recedes at the tip
and now, domesticated, it burns
harmlessly
so baby, next time we fight
please remember
i am the greatest lover among men
in and out of bed
and no matter how many frying pans
you raise to my head
i will always tuck you in
with that pink blanket
while we burn by the candlelight.

Rogue love

pink shirt
striped socks
with holes in them
lacey panties between my teeth
a pink decor of blossoms
and passionfruit
love on the altar
my name roared out
in godlike-fashion
my lips red-hot against
her stripped nakedness
sucking on her nipples
her thigh bones
her toes
her hair wild
covering the pillows
and the sheets
her arms arched
folded around my shoulders
gripping and clobbering my
back
hot spring visions in my brain
sweet brief euphemisms
the condensed insides of a snowflake

crystal balls dropping from
the heavens
shattering against painted
canvas
naked and done, we wrap
ourselves in sheets of
stained love

she walks to the bathroom
turns on the water
lets it run
i wipe off on the side

and the hours resume.

Listless

many of my dragging
arguments
with my girlfriend
are about how cold
and brooding I am
how static I tend to become
my body
hardens
with conflict
and my mind
cripples
and cramps up
i start to hear
my veins popping
and feel the hairs
on my head
gradually stand up.
i am no good
as a loving man
as a debater
as an engager
of wars.
i am listless;
a listless lover
in my works
in my passions

in my attitudes
there,
it is out now
with the butterflies
scattered in the rooms
and the little cats
scampering after them
clawing against the window
panes
and the cheap bathroom curtains
hanging in the main room
a listless boy
living a listless life
dull, inanimate living
slouching toward an uneventful end.
the cop cars still make their rounds
every 1 or 2 hours at night
and I think of Canada
of the cold
of the heat in the Gulf
of the endearment of Paris
and the library books
and the punched lunch cards
in my wallet (the tenth punch
gets you a free meal)
and the girls
with their pulled-back hair
swinging ponytails
dreaming of unicorn streams

of pink running river waters
to drink from
and swim in
and the last cigarette
smoked in baked grey shrouded
clouds of unfiltered air
exhales the bitter breath
of madness
dripping from my faucet.

Eyesore

baby,
if you are a shooting star
i am the milky way
if you are
a meteorite
i am your orbit
if you are
a celestial object
i am the cosmos
if you are star dust
i am the black hole
of enlightenment
if you are a vacuum
i am the strings
shaping up the universe
if you are a beam of light
i am a prism
absorbing
and diffusing
your rays
to the naked eye.

Madre

i have seen the pink cat
de-fossilized
resurrected
floating above the tall grass

Madre
waiting by the clock for 6:00 a.m.
to pack lunch bag

Madre
pure and unwary
oblivious to underhanded living:
absinthe shots lined on bartop
snorted and washed down with cocaine
gang-bangers dreaming still
of bigger orgies
in the middle of the city

Madre
picturing little boy
playing with toys on bedroom floor
extending influence on man
who hasn't learned to hold a razor
upright
badly-shaven face dotted with
sparse stubbles on the sides

weak man
frail man
but alright
Madre thinks
protected little boy
secured innocence
from big bad world of doom

Madre waiting
for Sunny engine car sound
in the driveway
waiting for subdued face of little boy
coming home from casual evening

unaware
of late-night busboy shifts
balancing plates on nose
spinning trays on finger
chasing great golden sun
of fluttering words

bad boy
anomaly

Madre refusing
bad writer roleplay gimmick
bad social practices
drinks and smokes
building hopes on shoulders of boy
cultivated from shadow of father

Madre
troubled
angling for respite
constant
in the good face of boy
injected with heroine shots
of pure life and danger
cultivating the streets at night
for education
blowing mother a sweet kiss on the forehead
before blowing off college
in search of the dream

Madre unknowing
caresses angel-headed son
cracking and breaking
interior
man wants out

Madre unknowing
sweet tender
unknowing
son too proud
to make her tearful
hides life's edge and daring
from her
stands by her
holds out warm hand
of love and care

Madre
I've outgrown dead father
buried last sentiment in his tomb
I've grown wings
too big for home
too big for
Madre

Madre whose tears
never left the bedside lamp
dark corners of prayer and memory
of resting everlasting peace
whose voice sneaks
under blanket on cold evenings
in laundry room
in phrases
sometimes

Madre
mother of life

Man
entering foray of new world
building debts and home
and bookcases for books
unwritten

unwritable

a last kiss on the forehead
departing
into the tall grass
where the pink floating cat waits.

Slowing down

winter in Paris
is slow
and slows everything
down
with it:
some days i even feel
old and doubt if i'll
make it out
of bed
(i barely do sometimes)
my girlfriend makes coffee
and i can spot the hot vapor
coming out
she lights a smoke
and the tip slowly burns red
i lean in and bite her

ear
she gets up
gets dressed
goes to work
comes back
several times
her papers
in a mass of heap
in one corner of the living room

i think about pulling myself
up and getting out
as well
but fail
i am a corpse
stitched to the wall
listening to the heavy drops
pounding outside

i orient myself
to the bedroom
where the typer sits
mighty
yearning for a good hand
but i show up weak
what good, i say, will it
do if i use it?
the pounding outside
accelerates
and intensifies
then goes into a trickery:
vanishing
then coming back harder
like false clarity
or a fly on the wall

the room darkens
the teapot boils and whistles
i resign myself
to the chair

the door clicks
unlocks

my woman
drenched from head to toe
like a great big splash of water
walks in and throws
more paper
on top of the heap.

Two eyebrows

a face
a mirror
a face
a spit
a grunt
backlash;
shower towel
around the waist
white walls
all around
shampoo bottles
bathtub
soap
water smoke
and pouf!
two eyebrows
looking back
hairy chin
cuckoo call
striking clock
sex in the laundry room
with the woman i
wake up next to
jazz music
all around
brings back the voice

of Kerouac
sitting next to Cassidy
chuckling
all of them
in boring poetry readings
university letters
flood the mailbox
i curse the mailman
death to the post office
death to the post office
my woman dries me off
and trims my mustache
my head sings
i am in love
i am in love
whoopie!

Sunday & rain

beer
the smell of candle
(red fruits)
i've never been a bully
her, kissing the sheets
with wet pink lips touching
against the white linen
naked
i've never been a nice guy
or liked or appreciated people much
outside, rain
mud and wet soil
dirty soles stamping
on the ground
i've preferred conversations
with dead men
and traded the living for books
peach blossom white bosom
peaking from under the sheet
her
in her red-coated glasses
perfumed in strawberry scented
grace
eyes scintillating
and the rain
it's Sunday

and the week turns
and another approaches
i adjust my seat
more beer
more vigor
more inspiration
i can write to you about dead heroes
or climate change
or the human condition
but instead i'll stick
with simple matters:
earlier today
we hung a poster
from the ceiling
that reads *Life is good*
right when the rain started
and it hasn't stopped
pouring ever since.

Mild conversation

there was this one
woman i dated once
that told me
i had communications issues
'you don't know
how to communicate,'
she used to say.
'you don't know
how to speak up
and express what's
inside of you!'
'okay,'
i said.
'you just keep
hiding
and hiding
things
and bury them!
also,
you're terrible
with women
you don't know
how to treat one!'
then she usually
picked up something
like a pack of cigarettes

and threw it against the wall.
look lady,
i have communication issues
i always sleep on one side
i've never read Dylan Thomas
and I am disgusted
by black widows
stuffing their faces
in chocolate cupcakes
on the metro.
i think revolutions
are pointless
and overstated
and i like to sit
in small coffee shops
and read
without buying anything.

how'z
that
for
communication?

The gut

everything starts
and ends
there.
there is a shortage
of metrics
for human beings
in giving, loving, receiving.
but i have broken
through
every and all
preservation;
i have broken through
it all.
now there is
the hysterical pleasure
a snow globe on the bed stand
shaking of happiness
and ecstasy
and bliss.
all the angel-heads
the crude
crass
unfortunate
inferior
leeches
grabbing onto human life

for another chance
gather at my doorstep:
i hear their banging
just now
as i stroke these keys
with my fingers.
it is there
the light is there
for the taking
once you've been in love
and have been living
under the shade of its
umbrella.

Diane,
wherever you are now
know that you have taken
the soul from this room
the age-old rotting face
stuffed in cheap salad bars
and liquor
and breathed kindness
into it.

How to be a poet

european winters
were hard and treacherous
but i say
don't be afraid of the northern wind
it brings peace

people are seldom
born as poets
the lucky ones
die knowing they were
but most
go on living
without knowing it;
thinking they were just
born anti-social
or cynical
or masochistic…

i seemed to write better love poems
whenever i was out of love
out of the game
out of it
instead of in it
my girlfriend
took most of the edge

out of me
and now
i wake up
and kiss her bosom
and watch the sun come up
over her naked body
while we make love
until the toaster clicks
and the microwave snaps
and breakfast is served in bed

we even play chess
together
and she reads off my lap
while i put on
the great composers
the great pianists
that we both love
listening to…

in the end
being mad
and being in love
are not so far apart
they both require
a transfiguration
of the soul
an outwardly leap

into that place
made out of crystal
and glass;
and as the shards regroup
to form solid ground
a stepping stone is born
and we traverse
we traverse endlessly
into untraceable boundaries
leaping, leaping
filling our hearts with joy
and getting drunk and mad
on laughter
waterfalls made of wine
and little hut houses with carved crescent windows
there is no better time
to be a poet
than when you are in love
no harder time
when you are not.

It starts from the end

it starts from
the end.
normally it's the pain
that flicks and tricks
in my guts before
spilling out
on the page.
but Monday mornings
aren't so gleam
anymore,
you know?

she wakes up
distraught and impatient
with the world
and i look at her
i really look at her.

she makes her own
smoke
smokes it
with her cup of coffee
and her face lights up
and the world
around her

lights up
too.

i still look at her
and inner peace
fills me.

she still hasn't said
a single word
but she gently runs
her hand
along my arm
and feels the little hairs
standing up

i've made love
to this woman
and documented
the nights
we shared
prowling each other's
backs
like flashes
in my brain.
i've hung her body parts
like little photographs
on a wire
in a dark room

i've been re-introduced
to the gods
the saints
the prophets
through her
by intimately entering
her body
and soul.
she's kept me off
the haze
the dirty dirty
haze
the filthy smoke
that followed me
and deconstructed me
night in
night out
across every channel
of my life.

now walking in
the fog
with no lights
the only beacon i see
is her name
flashing
flashing in sparkles

i've been
re-introduced
to life
to love
to feeling
feeling cuts deeply dissecting
my limbs
my raw lumbering limbs

because of her.

Snow

It falls through windows & walls
& we are in bed
our skins shedding
& we don't know when

the world will end
we don't know
when this city will end
when someone will pull
the rug from under it

& we are in bed
under a white sheet
her face
a first snowflake.

And we make love

and we make love
and we make love
in the darkest hours
of the night

as the pinned
reflections
of our shadows
against the wall
slowly anticipate
dawn.

Symbiosis

today i walk
today i walk
in the sun:
my woman
just caught
her train
and I am left
to enjoy the trail
of dust
gathered behind.
for the first time
the country
opens up
to me;
the joy of
the Christmas season
can be felt
in my heart –
the happiness
of the people
palpable
in my soul.
there is no room
for the damned;
no room
to curse

bad writing
or lacking inspiration
or tired cognitive
activities
there is no need
for shields
from the dark;
they have been thrown out
and the last clothes of winter
worn out
and put out on the cloth line
the little crows
approach me
but i close the window
i silence the walls
i turn off the stations
t.v, radio,
even the typer
the typer that has been
ever so good
to me
infusing my veins
with good precious
blood every once
in a while
producing delicious

material
for me to show off
to some street folk
or some cheap-shot editor

i shut it down
now
i shut it down
For a while.
it is quiet.
it is quiet
now
in this Christmas season
the festivities align
outside
the capital is shining
brimming with lights
bright lights all over
the people's faces

my phone rings:
it is
my woman
she tells me
her mother is visiting
her
i wish her luck
i wish her
the best of luck
just as i hope

some poor folk
on the street
wishes me
when he reads
these words.

Ruminations

i re-invent
her
and she
re-invents
me
as the shouters
in yellow jackets
outside
put chairs
and tables
through store fronts

you would like
to tell them
there are more
pressing things
in the universe

but instead
i look at her
i feel her soothing breath
and think of
serenity
of a new world
where we both belong
even for fractions

like a late late
partition
introduced
at the final stages
of a symphony

now I look
at the time
i look at the clouds
the curtains
the floor
and realize
i am not
entirely myself:
i am used to
feeding off
the vandalism
and uproars
of society
like a leech
for defiance
or what some call
artistry

but now
for a moment
i wish to have
nothing to do
with all of that
and simply bask

bask in the rainbow
leaping through my soul
and hers

i wish
to hang out
with the fools
and non-thinkers
for a while
to cater for
the stray cat
whose steps i can hear
down the alley

i wish to stretch
this moment
the same way
i would pause
and un-pause
a mystical song
in order to
keep up
with it

to push
the elastic limits
of my soul
to make
more room
for hers.

Manhattan

she called me Manhattan
and i was her star-crossed lover;
we cooked together
we slept together
we woke up together
we took the train together
heck,
we did everything
together

she called me Manhattan
and i was her star-crossed lover
and it took an entire city
to absorb
all the love
she had
to give.

Five

I wait for death Like a lover waits for love

critical thinkers

always an admirer
of critical thinking
man is still
a slave
to his senses:

he is slave
to the cook flipping burgers
in the fast food joint down the street

he is slave
to his boss-calling-cellphone
after-hours
deaf-tone ringing between his ears
during shower
dinner
sleep

he is slave
to his lover
who reels him to bed
after long work
or
on sleepy weekends
sleepless always

performing duties of love
and lust
tasting magnum lips
that clamp hard on his
making pink purple buff skin peels
washed down by whiskey
in a moment's aloneness

he is slave
to the glass
the pitcher
the keg
the bottle
the shot
the trigger
the expanding bullet
in his heart
clogging veins and arteries
drying out brain
functions

man is slave
to his senses
it's always been
in the books
and out there
in the wild

the critical thinkers
have accepted it

and the rest
still think
they can get out
alive?

Da Vinci had his demons

but when he drew up
his Vitruvian Man
he pictured something along the lines
of Nietzsche's Superman

nowadays
we have amounted to
fire breathers
glass and insect eaters
animal hunters

we wake up
into boredom and nothingness
mounted by a fear of firearms
and dreams gone sour

perhaps the Superman
is meant to remain a myth
or a
superstition?

acceptance

a little poem
can get to your head

one good piece of work
gaining widespread acceptance
can shatter the barrier
of hesitation
and unlock
the door to invincibility

suddenly
a mild headache
is feared for
like a tumor

any bodily pain
becomes a growing concern
and a mortal threat
to the immortal soul

but worst of it all
is the irreversible thought
of going back
to producing
average work

or falling off
the standard

and eventually
that

is
what really
kills you off.

Requiem

this world is a sickly thing
i am a desolate man
walking back and forth

to airports and bus stops
under heavy storms
and lightning bolts

i am a man of my word

i am a man of my lines
i get scoffed at
and threatened by the hanger

i am the saint you never wished for
i am a petty cryer
at house parties and terminal gates

i fear illness
i fear sin
i fear the shot of rush
in the vein
the pill under the tongue

the man

the woman
shacking in my house

leaving food drops on my carpet

the stock market
the mall shop discounts

in rich city quarters
i am the bat that roams at night

the dream within a dream
the extra spoonful of sugar in the coffee cup

a requiem for humanity

a jellyfish living off

the last drop of the ocean.

An account on human progress

minds infected
with sports games, tv series,
award shows
the holocaust of the human
brain
is complete:
aneurism
upon aneurism
abduction of the psyche
masturbation of the self
laying waste
to the teachings
of freud
gauss
descartes
shakespeare
sucking on mojito 7-up
and caramel bars
consuming Haribo
lemon cigarettes
Coca-Cola
and Red Bull
complete annihilation

of taste and depth

they are many
already
and gaining more and more
numbers

join them.

And finally

and finally
there is nothing left
to be saved
nothing for this world
to take
outside, it is just
death
it waits for no one
only the strong live
and get to ride
this fast fast
rollercoaster
normalcy
is the norm:
measured and scaled
on the ability
to tie a shoe
learning to shave
fitting into a job
occupying a slot in a parlor
parallel parking between 2 cars
no time to blink
or hesitate
no more roads to cross
or superimpose
over the ones that have already been drawn

some will bastardize me
accusing me of writing this
from the comfort of my small home
in the city of lights
in the voluptuousness and beatitude
of paris

well to those
i say: i am
a citizen of the world
like you

and it is all
just the same.

Free Speech

we have tried to build

a system of social structure
since ancient times
forgone anarchy

relinquished our idealists
banned our thinkers
we have mounted chains
and ladders
introduced chaos
to put in place
a pyramid of power
but it is lost
time is passed that now
the time for poll voting and ballots

and surviving riots is behind us
somewhere we have failed
in finding a suitable route
for organizing large crowds
of men, women and children
to ensure their prospering and development

and longevity

down now with the concept of power
abolish the mantra of the ruling class
or classes

no more being bullied into
the establishment of governors
and bureaucrats in charge
fiddling with the lives of the majority

the greatest governments of our time
have always treated their people
with respect and autonomy
provided of course
they kept voting for them.

the bandit

heavy hawk gliding above me
blood stains on my shoulders
i am crab-killing arturo bandini
down-and-out henry chinaski
milton's paradise lost
hamsun the starving wanderer
i have overcome the plague of death
conquered the heart of every widow
opened up the vessels of the world
caught hemingway's whale-fish

i am
in line
to become
the most sought-after literary persona
the most discussed and analyzed figure
between the lines

humble and sound of mind
i have proudly overachieved
carrying within me
the golden cups of my listed heroes
adding my own fragrance

yes
i have worshipped them
in earnest times

but while they are merely mentioned
i want posters
newspaper headlines
my name
thrown out and about
between kids and grandkids
in courtyards and ballrooms
and trailer parks
pinned all over the map

yes, yes, yes
i spent my time rubbing the lamp
for the genie to finally emerge

what's that now?
my wish is your command?
very well,
make me
king of the literary world!

Ascent

day 1
flash visions of blistering beams

a garbage man trotting
on his cleaning engine truck
between the columns of
the train station

smelling the filth
on every floor tile
he thinks himself
the noblest of professionals

no girlfriend
no wife
no parent-love

stone-henged against
the face of the earth
coming out of a fire dance
was so much easier
when done alone
relationships were tiring
and unnecessary virtues
like religion
or literary discussions
held in warm afternoon cafes

each person voicing
their opinion
and everyone leaving
with their own
at the end of it all.

Exile trail

it's hard for me
to find a place
to settle:
wherever i go
i can never find
a place of acceptance
or welcome.
the arabs are still fearful
for their souls,
they gear up
for the wrath of goblins
and ghouls
and desert gods;
too much faith and prudence
often make for a fragile backbone

over in europe they don't
understand most of what
i say or write
and never took a liking to it;
whatever streets i walk in
i am different from the others

slouching
marching heavily
and i accept it

growing up
i was never into
the football matches
i was never good at flirting
with girls or dating much
nor was i particularly interested
in academics
or chess
or trivia games
the only thing i was good at
was being quiet
and seeking spots
to sit alone

i felt solitude
was more beneficial
to me growing up
than playdates and prom
and sleepovers
and practical jokes
and video games
but now i hit an impasse
i'm directionless
walking aimlessly
in an open labyrinth
aware only that
they haven't created a place
for people like me yet:

- » demented but sufficiently conscious not to harm those around me
- » desperate but not enough for suicide
- » quiet but not quite to command total solitude

> there is a shift in the heart
> that makes the leap from
> sanity to insanity
> a cakewalk;
> a crossover;
> a romping toward the staircase
> of the gods;
> it declassifies
> a member of the human race
> and relegates him
> to his own realm
> where the laws are twisted
> and reconfigured
> to his suiting
> and that place
> collides
> with this world's ideals
>
> you see,
> it has no politics
> no religious deities or beliefs
> no weapons shipped for war
> no reward system

no economical structure

it is an infinite wall
of granite that keeps on
crumbling
and re-emerges like
a boulder of an island
on another side of the earth
this is a space
where many things are lost
and drowned
but where very few
individuals
can be found.

Done

i am done
writing interesting stories
and poems
for your simple
entertainment.
i am sitting at noon
watching the hot water maker
shake itself to plain death
my girlfriend says
i am undatable
and i have been wearing
the same underwear
for 4 days.
i dream of 30 women
i am fucking
one of which
was my high school crush
and the kitchen table
is dirty with spilled coffee beans
and leftover butter.
the candle in the middle of the room
is red-fruit flavored
and slowly melts
into a tiny beacon
of light
chasing away the shadows

and the little peaks of pain
winding down from my stomach
to my legs.
i still have to change
the light bulbs
in the bathroom
activate
the smoke detector
time 14 minutes
for the sauce
and flip the meat.
look,
you can keep sitting here
and reading more of this
or you can go outside
and run wild with the dogs
but life's much too short
to do both.

This is a sad poem

i could never write
sober
or happy
so i generally took it as
a good omen
when i sat down to type
and came out short.
there was a pleasant
security to the white page
that the therapists
don't tell you about:
write down your feelings
they told me
every time i stepped into
their office,
writing helps you!
they didn't know
writing
was all i did
when things got dark
and cringy
and nervous
and edgy

and i reached
a breaking point
a boiling plate
writing was there
to stop the end-all-be-all
of it
to tone it down
to calm down the loud
and heavy breaths.

i reproach them
for setting me off
like that
and bringing up those
memories for me
evoking heart-wrenching
sting rays
that left gaping holes
in me.

i also reproach them
for not being more supportive
and asking me instead
not to write things down
not to wander
into the alley of my self
the backdoor of an unsafe world
where there is little
to no chance of coming back
unscorched.

if i were one of them
i would very well advise
my patients
to open a blank page
and stare
at it.

Waiting in line

i am standing in line
with the rest of the clan
waiting to renew
my French papers
most of our life
is spent
either standing
or waiting.
our mothers
wait for us
to get out of the cradle
and stand on two feet;
we stand above
the graves
of the dead
waiting to exhale
another breath of life
waiting for the next turn
the next punch
the next hit.
we're jacked by this life
and we jack others into it
be it the grocery clerk
the priest behind the confessional door
or the track runner;
and now

here comes the officer lady
wearing her white latex gloves
waiting to inspect me
and i stand in line
and my face has a loud look
drawn on it
and the people around me
wait,
stand
and don't move.

No ordinary man

i could easily detach myself
from things that appealed
to most men:
love, sex, women
frolicking in nature
long trips down distant avenues
travel and lavish food
things that usually captivate
but that i often found
i did not need

i would gladly sacrifice them all
most times
just for peace and quiet
to be able to prolong my stare
into deep space
and shut down
for a while
that was the true blessing
for me
because all things come and go
you sleep like a hero
and wake up a wanted man
crucified and betrayed
by those who admired you
and pledged to support you

that was it
for Nietzsche,
for Sartre,
for Camus,
and for me
there wasn't much in this world
there wasn't much in the input
we had to contribute to it
and no matter how great the weight we pull
we will find
it can always be erased
entirely.

now the question i face is:
why bother maintaining
the things we have
if everything will be gone
and taken away
one day?
if our own life
will not outlast
most of them
why bother
preserving
what we are bound to lose?
i wish for the philosophers
i wish to dig them out of their graves
and sit among them
maybe in their long slumber

they had finally reached the conclusion
of our existence
or some kind of answer
to this vicious cycle
or maybe the answer
got to them
and usurped them
of their thinking;
maybe this whole life
is a bore
a series of bores
and death, finally,
is the biggest one of them
and in waiting for it
we can choose
to regress, endure
or fill up

and on that matter
i am unsure
where i stand.

Mr. Writer

o Mr. Writer
let me hang your coat
o Mr. Writer
can i take a picture with you?
o Mr. Writer
will you jump in bed with me?
having been called
that
for most of my life
after recent successful
(some might say clever)
book deals
i find it abusive
to be clamped down
by the tag:
they think once the writing's
done there's fame
and they are quick
to cling on to
that fame and associate themselves
with it.

well,
they are wrong
the writing
is never done

the cycle keeps spinning
the bedsprings keep bouncing
the voices keep getting darker
and more mad
the neighbors
more conceited and distant
the world shrinks
with shrieks and inhuman begging
the tumultuous soul grows
more restless
and scoffs at library meetings
book signings
interviews
magazines
popularity
billboards
movie deals
agents
literary agents
more agents
competing for the next name

but the writing is never finished
we are finished
our labels are finished
our image of grandeur
and menace are washed away
but the writing
keeps going.

It takes something special

… to patent a lifestyle:
to set an alarm clock
and wake up
every day
at the same hour
and drink the same
pre-heated coffee
in the microwave
(3 cubes of sugar)
and chomp on
the same cereal box
that seems endless
from the day you bought it.
it takes something special
to pick up the same phone
dial the same numbers
make the same jokes
listen to the same complaints
drive around in the same car
stop at the same traffic lights
look at the same parcs
and museums
and restaurants
and cabarets
fill out the same paperwork
and march down to the post office

smile at the same old grimly lady
that 70-year-old bat that hisses at you
while filling and filing the envelope
walk down the same alleys
the same trashcans
talk to your psychiatrist friends
attend the same job
punch the same time clock
head back to the same apartment
with the same crusty floor
get into the same bed
with the broken springs
reset the alarm clock.

Biographies

this writer
was featured
in 7 interviews
but wait
that writer
was published
in 17 magazines
all over Europe!
but wait, wait
this one
right here
once worked
on a collaborative poem
with William Styron!
and that one
was on national tv
and they even let him
sing the national anthem
during the segment!
and what about you?
well,
what about me?
what have you done?
where have you been?
what are YOUR CREDENTIALS?
oh, well, you see

i've had a few POETRY
books published
here and there
they made it across Europe
and i've worked the novel
had a couple out too
but other than that
i've never really
rated myself

and i guess when it comes to having experience
in drawing up false aspirations
and pretentiously presenting myself
as an important worker of words
then i have none.

U.F.O

while the scientists
are busy excavating Mars
for life
i have stumbled
on another
scientific
miracle:
the discovery
of flying saucers.
yes, yes,
it's true
and i assure you
one of them
landed by my ground floor room
parked outside
by my overstretched window
and a band of aliens
3 little green men
came in
and started sniffing my walls
examining my dish pans
inspecting my shades
and chasing after the cobwebs
in the corners.
one of them
tells me

my coffeepot's empty
yes, i tell him,
i ran out of coffee.
the other one
tells me
my toothpaste
has gone dry.
i left the tube
open for too long,
i say,
and forgot where i placed
the cap.
the third one
tells me
my publisher
has been calling me
non-stop
for the past two weeks.
we're still trying to figure out
how to get my book
in bookstores in the Middle East!
i yell at him.
they are fine visitors,
a bit strange,
but fine visitors
they are quiet
don't make much noise
or ruckus
and seem to understand me

better
than most human beings.
when they were finished
with their snooping
and inspections
and prepared themselves
to leave
i asked them,
hey,
say there,
do you happen to need
one more
in your species?
i have a feeling
you could use a fourth!
they looked at each other
with their large mutant eyes
buzzed around a few incomprehensible
syllables
and politely nodded to me,
NO.
i saluted them
and they left.

good visitors they were,
indeed,
and they didn't even touch
my alcohol.

The new breed

desperate to break out
and get noticed
they try to mix up
various genders and forms
of art
like this one guy
who was a pianist
decided to mix
contemporary folk songs
with Schubert
atrocious
torturous to listen to

they think the way to art
is paved with glory
and chance
they play it like a hook
and if you can grab on
then you can almost certainly
rattle your way to the top

but they forget
that the faster
you try to get there
the quicker you'll die.

Shapeshifting

Rimbaud captured the crowd
with his spit-fire poetry:
most called him sensitive
but i always viewed him
as an oracle
with his ability to magnify
the little things
and make them BIG
to me that was the true
hallmark of a great artist.

now an ant walks up my dining table
and wouldn't you know
it almost looks like
a dragonfly.

Photograph

i photograph early mornings
in bed
flipping through the pages
of a poetry collection
going over every poem
trying to re-write it
and comparing mine
to the original
ah, fuck;
this morning is tired
the coffee cup is tired
the cereal bowl is tired
the poetry collection is tired
and irked by my meek and tired ways
our breaths are tired;
we waste our tired breaths
as the steamboats cross the river
followed by a swarm of ducks
and the antelopes
galloping away
hopping in the green meadow
that has yet to know death.

The only greatness

the only kind
of greatness
i found
in humanity
was its ability
to exaggerate
everything:
it exaggerated
its heroes
it exaggerated
its love
it exaggerated
its merchandise
it exaggerated
its tragedy
it exaggerated
its life
it exaggerated
its death.

Quarrel thoughts

old Van Gogh
took the gun out and put
a bullet in his stomach
Hemingway did it, too:
he took the gun and
planted a shot
in his skull.
i sometimes think about it
i think about
the feel of the magnum
in my hand
but to be truthful
i never dared
take it out of the drawer
it might be good
at laying to rest
the maddening haunting
calls
similar to what you hear
on deck
on a shipwreck
during a fatal storm
but mine are still manageable
containable
and i prefer to let them out
take them with me instead

make them smell the fresh air…

i was sitting at a small table
at a French restaurant
and i overheard
an American father
talking to his little girl
about Napoleon:
yes, you see,
he had two wives,
the first was Josephine,
and the second,
the second…
the second
I CAN'T remember
her name but he had two wives
all right!

then the daughter
asked him
how Josephine died
and he told her
then she asked him
how Napoleon died
and he said:
no, nah-uh,
he didn't

but everybody dies, daddy, she said
not Napoleon,

not to the French people
at least

and did you know
that in Spain
a matador
refused to battle
a bull
and made a reverence
to him
instead?

I dreamt I was scaling Notre-Dame

… stone by stone
boulder by boulder
my slippery naked soles
gripped against every rock
looking down
as the ground becomes smaller
as my body becomes higher
as the food stains and sauce drippings
on my shirt
pass through the clouds

wondering
who will catch me
if i were
to let go?
under there
underground
i will come crashing through
some platform
where regulars wait for
the subway train
i will fall under a ceiling
of decorated names
of artists and painters
made famous in Paris:
my body will fall and crash

and land on the hard granite
and my bones will crack
as my eyes look at the sky of names
Hugo
Verlaine
Rimbaud
Baudelaire
all written in glitter
towering above tourists
and civilians
rummaging about
forgotten hats and expensive souvenirs
losing pace with the turn of time
as the flapping wings of the last museum
housing the last of humanity's minds
and souls
fail to take off
and stir the crestfallen obedient puppets
hypnotized by luxurious photographs
and satin dresses
and culinary workshops
and horse rides in the countryside

i scale the heights of Notre-Dame
over the burning summit that had been forgotten
and never fixed
over the watchful gargoyle eyes
moving with the movement
of my limbs

across the spider webs that have not been cleaned
the cathedral bells left unheard
the prayers unanswered
the cracking spears
the faltering pillars

the bearers of time
discussed
a homage
to this great architectural sanctum
housing infinite wisdom
but their discussions
so light
fluttered like the cool spring winds
unto the skies
that my hands now touched.

I saw the face of god

on a storefront
selling second-hand computer hardware
hard drives, disks, keyboards on display
i walked by and saw god peeking through the window
looking in disapproval
at the street full of rowdy people
coming and going
buying and selling
advocating war and protesting against peace
he called out the hippies but they wouldn't answer
he called out the politicians but they pretended not to hear
he called out the stray cats and dogs and they came to him…

i saw the face of god
on the windshield of my car
coming back from a long day at the office
unbuttoning my shirt
loosening my tie
he stared at me and laughed
and quoted Sartre:

Hell is not other people
Hell is all of mankind!

he sneezed at my windshield
and i had to force a hard right
off the highway and into the woods

i saw the face of god in the mud
in a swamp full of dead wood and leaves
shed by the forest trees
i walked by him and tripped and fell
and splattered my face right into him

i got up and wiped my eyes
and saw the world in red:
skies being raided by air crafts
and carriers dropping bombs on hospital roofs
and school yards
gunned mercenaries breaking out into a parking lot
resisting long enough before surrendering and
taking turns
shooting each other
until the last one
who watched his brothers in arms all die
one by one
put a bullet in his mouth
and pulled the trigger
while shouting the name of god.

i saw flags being raised and waved up high
but they were not the flags of humanity
only tyrants
and the land being razed

by a beam of fire

then it went all dark
and the face of god returned
calling me to see more
and i refused
and i pushed it away
and i covered my ears and my eyes
and my stomach twisted and wrenched and
turned
and
turned

and god was gone
and the visions were gone
and the flags were gone
and the land was gone
and i was gone

until i returned
to the storefront
and looked for the face of god
and it
was not
there.

My place

trying to fight off
visions of a dystopian world
hanging at the cliff's edge
flooded by people
more and more populations
scrambling for a corner to stand in
no place whatsoever for me
to exist in it;
i dimmed the lights
and looked at my work
nicely furnished on the dining table
in front of me:
an ashtray
of unfinished cigarette butts
a half-eaten slice of pizza
now rotting in the sink
and the portraits of giants
figures that stamped their ideas
on pages and pages
now decked in my shelves
staring at me
whispering their little thoughts
of the man sitting here

the lone survivor of his breed
i watch my work
admire it
i've built my world
i've reserved a patch of green grass
on the great holy land
i can proudly call my own

the world can end
in a great blast of inferno
in a ballistic tornado
of thunder and fury
in a great big bang

i've found my place
and i can continue to kick
in it.

What I want to say

what i want
to say here
is that we've learned
our lesson
well:
we know
how to crunch
numbers,
we know
how to rob,
kill,
compute taxes
and then some.
our values are
ever-changing
they are hardly
even recognizable
and can't be put
into words
much less on paper.

we've burned enough holy books
to become all-knowing
philosophers
who preach death
and raucousness

we are the degenerates
of our time;
the photographing
animal-slaying
brute
ferocious
wildlings
detrimental and proud
and we attribute our weaknesses
and sicknesses
to mind pain
to lack of accessibility
when really
we are suffering
from ignorance.

some say
i have a writer's heart
and some even think
when the few good
men and women die
humanity
will weep
and lose a fragment
of its essence;
but i now wait in
the shadows
for death,
like the rest of them.

i wait for death
like a lover waits
for love

alone in his room
fondling a piece of
curtain
or by the train tracks
kicking pebbles
under the sun.

Six

Life is no more than a song performed in an open garden

Biting on my nails in the dark

biting on my nails
in the dark
as the last movie is screened
as the last poet writes down
his line
as the last mother
giving birth in a cold hospital bed
exhales
releasing her offspring
as the dead roses on death avenue
circling the deserted parlor
preach to the corpses
as the dog chases its tail
and mine in the street markets
as the soldiers hide in their tents
and cover themselves behind the backs of
defenseless citizens

biting my nails in the dark
the candlelight fills the air
the last scented candle
about to be extinguished
the pianist on my radio
still coming up with the goods
still producing the odes
my crippled hands are unable to

biting my nails in the dark
making love
to the woman who carries me
when my legs no longer want to
when my body rejects this world
this life
this light
under sweet aromas
and slightly salted lips

as the last dying roach
lying there on its back
in the kitchen corner
is forgotten.

A moth in the park

it's 5.00 p.m.
still no luck
out in the cold
the apartment dreary
teenage boys cutting in front of me
to do their laundry
and smoke hash
on the dryer
i have a supermarket list
but no money
my stomach is growling
but i can't think about food

baby, it's cold
but i can see a moth
a little orb of yellow light
floating in the air
from one lamp post
to another

i observe it
from the park bench
the cold wood
freezing my prancing ass
i remember how much you like
moths

how highly you speak of them
because they are attracted by the light
just like you
you say you would like to be reborn
as one
now that i watch it
now that i pay close attention
to this moth
i think
they are not bad
after all
hehe
little flashing creatures of the night
little candles floating until first light

candles
like the candle set you always have
on your dining table
vanilla-scented
that's another thing
you really like
candles bringing together
sight and smell
reconciling the senses
i admire your senses
your sensuality
your erotic naked raw vulnerability
dripping emotion
dripping on the wet shower floor

all the way to the bedroom…

i think that
all in all
i would like to be
a moth
tonight;

that wouldn't be
such
a terrible
thing.

The sound of the hummingbird

oh, i am a dangerous man
i stagger slowly across the cracking
dusty floor
with the lamplight turned on
(the main light has been broken
since i moved into the place)
open the cupboard
and take out a can of tuna

i count the stack of remaining
cans:
4
cans of tuna
for the end of the week

the fridge gurgles and roars
and i give it a little kick to shut
it up
it's dysfunctional
and it's been giving me signs
that it's waning
and so i don't rely on it
too much
or even too little

i have my cans of tuna
to last me
the end of my days
just like the sagging mattress
they bought for me
when i moved in
and placed it on the half-assembled
bed
to make sure
i would be comfortable

oh, i am a dangerous man
with all this havoc
my fingers still get numb
for the word
my soul still searches for the way out
on the page

oh, i am a dangerous man
the hot water don't come
so i take my showers cold
and wrap 2, 3
towels over my chilling body

oh, oh,
i am a dangerous man
a dangerous man
still sending out poems

by the dozens
every week
emailing every publishing press
magazine
in France and in the US
the post is too slow
for me
so i send them out the window
i send them flying
and they float over the clouds
some of them even get stuck there
or get caught by some tree
or the Eiffel tower
or land on one of those tour boats
on the Seine

oh, i am a dangerous man
i feed the little termites
that keep me company at night
sometimes when the bed's too hard
and i opt for the floor

i watch them live off me
and the little bits of food
i throw at them
unconcerned
by payments

sustainability
responsibilities
not trying to wear the system
or fit into it
that must be nice

oh, oh, oh
i am a dangerous man.

Last days

the last days
will be spent
curled up in a library
with a heavy blanket

going over
the immortal books
that will be here
long after us.

About the dead and the dying

the forecast says
it is the hottest it has ever
been in the history of Paris

the radio calls it
hell in Europe
people are burning
walking like flammable sticks
roasted alive

the heat
and the city
are unforgiving
and i watch the lively souls
burn from my window
with the fan on

even the flies
can't make it:
but even they know
that the dead are gone
dormant in their tombs
while this life lays waste
to the dying.

Hush now

hush, now
little girl
naked in bed

we are burning
in flames
the flames
of ourselves

there is nothing
except you
me
and Chopin
banging on his piano

you hold my hand
and tell me how powerful
my name is

my name that
i never liked
or used
even when i wrote my books
and poems
and other things

you tell me
you are cold
and ask me to close
the window
without leaving your side
without leaving you.

I am the warmth:
you are the delicate
sheath trembling
in my arms

vibrating
across the room
bouncing against the walls
pinging my spine
back
and forth
back and forth

and the window still
lets in the cold
inviting a world
that wouldn't dare
disturb our peace

and we forget the window
and we forget the cold
and we forget the dirty dishes
on the sink

and the flames of every burning cathedral
multiplying within us
and your scream
your gasp
your word
is all
i long for.

Where is my mind?

here we are
tip-toeing again
into nothing
the car washed
the trash taken out
the mail brought into the house
slumping
into a new-familiar automation

i go looking for it
in the innocent eyes
of young girls in summer clothes
or on football fields
where the grass is always green
even in winter

the great books
give me no answers;
they tell me
the same things
i already know:
that the writers back then
had more flair
soul
they were more
real

than now
now pretenders
soil this great art
that i adore
and live for.

shacking with my girlfriend
we still argue
over pancakes
or sandwiches
or breakfast
tearing at each other
before jumping in bed
and making love
again

it lingers
on a fine electric wire
next to the brown bird
the youngest of three:
brown
red
black

they share the wire
with my mind
and the occasional current
that slips through
zaps them
until they fly away

and gives me a kind of shock
that releases me
from my habitual self

every day
is a struggle
a search
for that piece of me
now defunct
almost
petrified
fit for the museum
but i go on
spurred
by onlooking strangers
everyday civilians driving their vehicles
or buying their groceries

who, like me,
are searching too.

Payout

received
an email
today
from my publisher
with an attached sheet
of my sales
report
for the past
month

wincing
my ageing
wrecked eyes
i go over
the numbers:
10 paperback orders
5 online orders
5 misc. orders
a total
of 20 copies
sold
and my share
of the royalties
figuring in a little
cell box
at the bottom left

of the sheet

now i can
proudly
disclose
that i am
7$
richer
than i
was
this morning.

E-mail

"while we've thoroughly
enjoyed reading
what you sent us,
unfortunately
we will not
accept it
for publication
this time".

i got another
comical reply
from a publisher
this morning
this time
in the heart
of Paris.

i'm happy to say
by now
i made it a habit
to have at least
one rejection
per city

Beirut,
Paris,
Barcelona,
Rome

maybe London
is next
on my list?

hey,
i might even
become
the most-internationally-acclaimed
rejectionist
in the world

a truly
global
phenomenon.

Performance

there she is

running around
in a garden of leaves
green, brown, yellow
holding up an old tree branch
like a microphone pole
grabbing it by the tip
and singing out loud
to some 90's rock music
she looks at ease

at ease as if
the garden
was her stage.

i sit afar
far enough
to observe her
one minute
holding a book
in my hand
the other
coloring a few pages
with words

But never
taking my eyes off
her.

her soul flashes
in front of me
and the image
of the daunting tiger
fades in my mind.
the image
of the nasty foul world
dissolves
in my mouth
like a bad aftertaste
you get rid of
by spitting out.

seeing her
break free
seeing her
caress the grass
lie on it
try out her blue sunglasses
in the sun
makes me realize
how simple
things really are;
or rather

how foolish
we people
are made to look
for complicating them.

life
is no more
than a song
performed
in an open garden.

Novels

today another attempt
at a novel
ended in the
dust bin.
that raises my total count
to 35:
34 attempts
and only 1
that has seen the light

and in the wake of this
i'm left wondering
where all the talent
has gone
or if it has been present
from the start?

or was it just
an emotional outburst
or a spike that started
at the gut
and ended
on the page?

with each passing day
the margin on my white paper
thickens

and i feel like putting myself back
on the drink
or shitting everywhere
or doing
unholy things

anything to prevent
this descent
this fall

to push back the spears
on the empty shelves
threatening me

oh, ever threatening me!

Blue morning

sitting here
in a small coffee shop
across the street
from the
university

the campus
is Parisian;
the accents
are Parisian;
the coffee
is Parisian;
the street tiles
are Parisian;
the music is
Parisian;

reading one
of the greats:
an American genius
billed and labeled
mad and washed-up
by average citizens

i reach a point
where I force myself
on the pages

you see,
even the great books
can be difficult
to read

but being
in that world
being transported
back to
San Pedro
in the 70's
seeing places
you've never seen
meeting people
you've never known

you realize
with time
the priorities
change
but the madness
stays the same.

Post office (or Tribute to C.B.)

today
a woman
was mailing
a letter
at the post
office.
she stared at
the yellow bin
for a good 2 minutes
before making up
her mind:
France | International
read the sign.
she inhaled,
exhaled the frosty
french air
and slid the envelope
in the left slot.

i went to the post
office to pick up
a parcel.
the officer
gave me the mean look
for coming in early
but otherwise

the atmosphere was
as quiet
and subdued
as you would expect
from any regular
Monday morning.
they'd sent me
a copy of
my latest book
from the States.

i looked at it
felt the skin of it
leafed through the pages
took a whiff
out of the paper.

it was good
good to see
the words falter
and fall out
of the pages
slowly
then hit hard
and plummet
at the bottom.

it has been
35 days
since I last
wrote

and
according
to this book
in my hand
i still
haven't
lost it.

Madmen

i am
half-man
half-century;
i never really
understood
society;
paintings
never spoke
to me;
people
don't affect me
they zero in
zero out
while i prowl
in and out
of the dark;
the jails
the judges
the police
the army
the law
are designs
constructs
boundaries
meant to hold things
together

but they keep me back
they weigh
me down

Bukowski
was slammed
The Beats
were hated
Dante was punished
Hamsun was slated
Hemingway was paraded
in chains on city streets

why am i choosing
to tell
you this

all this
to say
the true
never live
until
they go mad.

Railway poetry

but we fight
and we fight

but i want her
to know
that all the daggers
i've stuck into her
all the whips
all the lashing outs
we exchanged
and the forced contacts

did nothing
to shake or
disrupt
the stillness
i consider her
to be

as for my image
i hope to see it
reflecting in the pigments
of her eyes
like i am used to now

or maybe
i will go looking for it

picking it up
assembling it from the bottom
of some drained glass
of wine
after she is done
with it.

First dream

i had a dream
about her
last night
woke up
in a pool
of sweat
and leftover
whiskey stench

the night
was banging
on my door
again;
but the vision
of her
in my dream
wearing a purple top
a black blazer
and playing with her
loose hair
put the demons
at ease
for some time.

she was caressing
my features

and i was
breathing
in her face
like i always
naturally
did

seeing her
in the haze
of my memory
evoked
the safe house
the haven
the playground
only she knew
how to provide
for me

there are many things
there are many things
i should tell you
there are
many
things i have
to tell you

but for the first time
playing writer
doesn't seem to
cut it;

the word-blade
has lost
its edge
the word-firecracker
has lost
its crackle
the river
has hit
a dam

but as i scratch
my head
in darkness
i realize
words
are still
my allies;
and i will
keep pushing them
shoving them
through the wormhole
of the world

but here is the secret
here is the deepest secret
that comes crawling
from the corners
of the room
or perhaps
the underlings

of my soul
and that secret
is truth

truth
that now stands
between me
and the world
truth
that now stands
between
me
and
you

truth
that i will carry on
to the battlefield
to burn down
massive fortresses

truth
that will hit
like a series
of rapid-fire
missiles
and silence
all the lies

truth

that will cleanse
me
and rid me
of the hesitations
i've tirelessly
set up

truth
that will force
its way
through your walls

truth
that will explode
and splatter
across
the pages
of a child's
coloring book

truth
that will
bring back
hazelnut fillings
to your eyes.

New beginnings

but we tiptoe
into new beginnings
caught between the sails
of the past
the rapid waves
of the future
searching for the lighthouse
or the traveling seagull
to guide us
to familiar shores
trusting that
morning coffee and music
hot shower water
and early conversations
are things
we can marvel at
and delight in
again.

Broke men on broken platforms

they carried
their scripts
and paperwork
and letters
marshalled by
the credence
of reward and survival
of maintaining failed marriages
that almost solely relied
on getting the kids fed
dressed
and educated

they spend night shifts
hopping from one platform
to the next
changing destinations
sparing a cent or two
whenever they can
to the poor entertainers
singing in train wagons
and playing their instruments
thinking maybe
just maybe
someone or something
up there

will repay the favor

in desperate need of living
and believing in the way of life
they no longer think
that it is in their hands
and let it flutter away
terribly
sadly
carried by the wounded wings
of destiny.

First sunlight

i wake up next to her
as the chirping of
the little birds
outside
blows into my ears
the silent city sleeps;
but every breath she draws
and exhales
on me
makes me feel
awake
and
alive.
i think of
whatever has anchored me
to my principles
to my loneliness
to my distrust
and faithlessness
in another human soul

it has run away
it has run away like dogs
it has run away like mad days
it flees like blackbirds

perched from the end of the tree branch

        i need her
        i need her
        were the words
        that failed to see
        the first sunlight.

Into the night

spending
sleepless
nights
exhausting
lifecycles
lifetimes
making up for
all the wasted breaths
all the restless throbs
as the wind bellows and bangs
against the upper window

we ask ourselves
where broken things
have been and gone
astray
how the things
we spent lifetimes
losing
suddenly
come back.

My whole life

my whole life
has been
a series of

missteps;
brief moments
between mistimed
events
of telling the wrong
women
i loved them
and the right ones
nothing
at all.

My landlady

coming home
from work
to find a pinned
note
on my door
from the landlady:

U'R LATE
WITH THE RENT
AGN.
NEXT TIME
I'LL THRO
U OUT!!!

i took off
my clothes
went in
for a quick shave
grabbed a beer
and stared
as the clock
struck 6.

A ray of hope

we would be
young
and mad
and in love
and take
hot showers
together
and in the midst
of the steam
i would plant
kisses
on your head
repeatedly
for the number
of times
i've loved you
while my heart
slowly opens up
to the possibility
of hope

for this wreckage
for the upcoming days
and for myself.

Reverence dance

she is not
here now
but i am in front
of her picture
a portrait that
hangs beside the saints
and the mercenaries
and the gods.
there is no time
for worshiping;
worshiping won't
cut it
this time
nor will the fallen
tears on the lawn
on cold afternoons.
the sirens outside
my window
remind me
there are more important
things
to worry about
than simply
being alive
or surviving.
the silent

radio sets
and tv stations
are a testament
to our own fear:
the fear
of turning them on
and watching the carnage
the famine
the death counts
in third world countries
in our streets
in our homes.
we run.
we run
and turn it off
to exclude ourselves
from the truth:
we would like
to spend our lives
worrying
about the cleanness
of our rooms
about paying our taxes
on time
about the jobs we hold
and the slips we receive
at the end of the month
about the shopping malls
and bars where we can

blow off steam and revenue
about a love pursuit
and finding the person
that is made solely
for us
but the truth
is much worse
the truth is bitter
and ugly
and cold
in the form
of unresolved
hunger
missile launch pads
shelter-less casualties
and lack of awareness

i am still
in front of her
picture
the picture
of a girl
staring at me
with the biggest eyes
her soft lips
eclipsing the weak rays
of sunlight
desperately
pushing through

the cloud storm
to penetrate
my dark sanctuary;
they are almost
touchable
and so is she
and i am ashamed
ashamed that in this moment
my words
are more powerful
than my thoughts
they express the degenerating
state of mankind
the retrograde motion
of the planet
while my thoughts
slip away again
to that green paradise
closing into a mountain top
where i am alone
with her
drinking a hot cup
of coffee
inhaling
the sunlight
her head
planted against
my waist
her giggles

like ripples
in my stomach
and to only have that
worry
in mind
is more than
ideal
but still
very far
from the state
of how
things
really
are.

Betting on the human race

i have faith
in humanity
almost as much
as i have faith
in the eternal
being.
we are promised
rose buds
and golden leaves
but always end up
sucking burnt crop
like dead straws.

Out-sped by a machine

my words
are heavy;
my writing
machine
is a tombstone.
outside
they are
experimenting
with new
technology
that can produce
great art
breeding
mechanical
things
capable of writing
books
just like us
if not
better
than us.
i wonder
if we will ever

witness
the day
where they will
hold a woman's hand
endearingly
or love
better
than
us.

From the book of the greats

perpetually walking
in reverse
against the flow
of the masses
opposite the direction
of the crowd
erasing time
and space
where they have
created them ⊠
writers of the past
have warned us
about the dangers
of taking too similar
or trivial paths
and today
their advice
still holds true

i walk
constantly
in reverse
of the crowd:

wherever they go
i take the alternate way
to get there first?

no,
but at the very least
to get
somewhere.

My melancholia

each one of us
carries a
speck
of the human
suffering
be it
the bachelor
banging
his head
against the
apartment
wall
or the woman
waiting in line
at the grocery store
or the beggar
holding his cup
hoping for a penny
or two
or the drinker
trading the madness
for a few moments of scotch
or the group of girls
backpacking through
ancient cities
of forgotten lore

each human being
has it ingrained
in the garden
of the soul

the human suffering
the eternal strife
that comes with the
excessive outreach
the waxed wings we use
to elevate ourselves
and touch the bright light
always striving
always looking up
always soaring to the clouds

and even those
collecting the accolades
handing out free speeches
to the hopefuls
never truly bury
that seed.

Big city life

broke and poor
in a big city
i went to the
libraries
to read books
i couldn't afford
visited closed art galleries
on Sundays
to admire
the few pieces
on the display
window
took long
strolls
in the park
watching on
the children of
the sun
chasing their rubber
ball
without asking
for their names.

Manifesto

Da Vinci
Picasso
Michelangelo
discovered
the secret
to immortality:
it lies
on the canvas

that is where
life is channeled
from the body
when it can
no longer
carry on.

Poetic outlaws

we are here
to drink beer
we are here
to write
good poetry
messy poetry

we are here
to be submerged
by a weird helpless
hatred
for writing
without having written
anything

we are here
to choke on
the aspirations
of the living
to make a mockery
out of the threat of dying
to sit in our closed
circle
and wait for the universe
to begin
and end
before us.

www.ingramcontent.com/pod-product-compliance
Lightning Source LLC
Chambersburg PA
CBHW071335080526
44587CB00017B/2845